NATURE WATCH

AMERICAN BISON

Revised Edition

Written by
Ruth Berman

Lerner Publications Company • Minneapolis

In memory of Michelle Helen Berman
And for all animals struggling to survive in
our ever-shrinking natural world – RB

Special thanks to Dr. Al Steuter, Director of Science
and Stewardship, Niobrara Nature Conservancy, for
sharing his knowledge of bison and the prairie. Thank
you also to the staff of the Northern Trail of the
Minnesota Zoo and to Russ Sublett and the others at
the Minnesota, Nebraska, and Dakota field offices of
the Nature Conservancy.

Lerner Publications Company
A division of Lerner Publishing Group, Inc.
241 First Avenue North
Minneapolis, MN 55401 U.S.A.

Website address: www.lernerbooks.com

Library of Congress Cataloging-in-Publication Data

Berman, Ruth.
    American bison / by Ruth Berman. — Rev. ed.
        p.   cm. — (Nature watch)
    Includes bibliographical references and index.
    ISBN 978–0–8225–7513–9 (lib. bdg. : alk. paper)
    1. American bison—Juvenile literature. 2. American bison—
History—Juvenile literature. 3. West (U.S.)—History—Juvenile
literature. I. Title.
QL737.U53B48 2009
599.64'3—dc22   2007030530

Manufactured in the United States of America
1 2 3 4 5 6 – DP – 14 13 12 11 10 09

CONTENTS

Bison are the largest North American land mammal.

INTRODUCTION

DARK FORMS BLACKEN THE HORIZON. DUST RISES HIGH IN the air. The earth begins to shake. A dull, faraway sound settles into a rhythm. The dust cloud looms closer and closer. The rhythmic rumble gets louder and louder. Soon the noise can't be separated from the trembling of the earth. A black wave of huge, shaggy animals with thundering hooves explodes across the treeless plains.

The plains bison fed and clothed the Plains Indians as well as the pioneers as they traveled west. And the plains bison became a symbol of the American West. This is their story.

Like American bison, cape buffalo from Africa *(above)* and highland cattle from Scotland *(opposite)* have horns.

BISON
OR BUFFALO?

FOR MANY YEARS, PEOPLE HAVE CALLED BISON "BUFFALO"
by mistake. Many believe this confusion started when early French
explorers first saw American bison. The explorers were reminded of
their own cattle, which they called *boeufs* (buh). The British settlers had
difficulty saying this French word. In time, the word came to be pro-
nounced "buffalo." There actually are animals called buffalo *(above)* living in Asia and Africa. The bison and buffalo *are* members of the same
scientific family. But the two animals are quite different. American bison
are more like our domestic cattle than they are like true buffalo.

In spite of the confusion surrounding its name, there is no mistaking
the American bison. Its silhouette alone distinguishes the bison from any
other animal. Most distinctive is the bison's hump. It is made of muscle
and bone that extends from the spine.

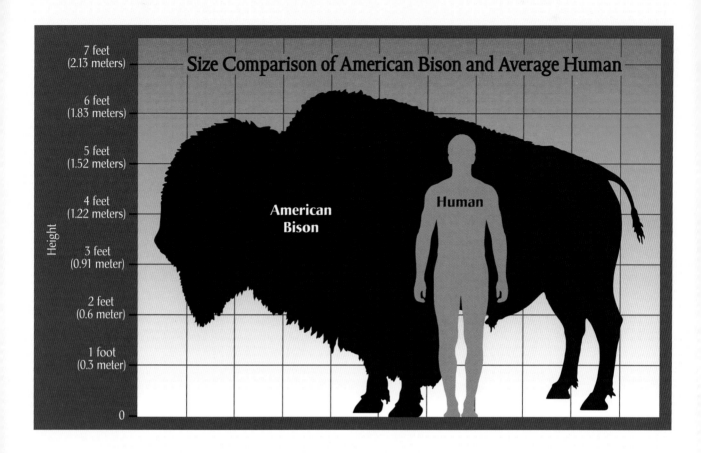

Size Comparison of American Bison and Average Human

Height

7 feet
(2.13 meters)

6 feet
(1.83 meters)

5 feet
(1.52 meters)

4 feet
(1.22 meters)

3 feet
(0.91 meter)

2 feet
(0.6 meter)

1 foot
(0.3 meter)

0

American Bison

Human

The bison's hump helps support its huge head. The hair on the hump and on the bison's whole front end is two to five times thicker than the hair on the rear end. This adds to the bison's unusual and imposing appearance. An adult male, or **bull** can weigh up to 2,000 pounds (900 kg). An adult female, or **cow**, can weigh more than 1,000 pounds (450 kg). Bulls grow to be about 6.5 feet (2 m) tall. And cows are only slightly shorter. That makes bison the largest North American land mammal.

RELATIVES

The American bison's ancestors, or relatives, came to North America from central Asia. They came thousands of years ago, during the last ice age. Much of the water in the world had frozen into giant sheets of ice. These ice sheets are called glaciers. The glaciers made the level of the sea drop by nearly 400 feet (120 m) in some places. The shape of the land was changed. One newly exposed stretch of land crossed the Bering Strait. It connected Russia to an area that is part of modern-day Alaska. The bison's ancestors were among the many animals that walked across this land bridge. Then they moved across North America.

There are two **subspecies**, or kinds, of American bison. Their common names are plains bison and wood bison. But scientists have their own way of classifying animals. They give every kind of animal a special scientific name in Latin. That way, people the world over are able to recognize each animal by its scientific name. The plains bison has the unimaginative scientific name of *Bison bison bison*. The wood bison is called *Bison bison athabascae*.

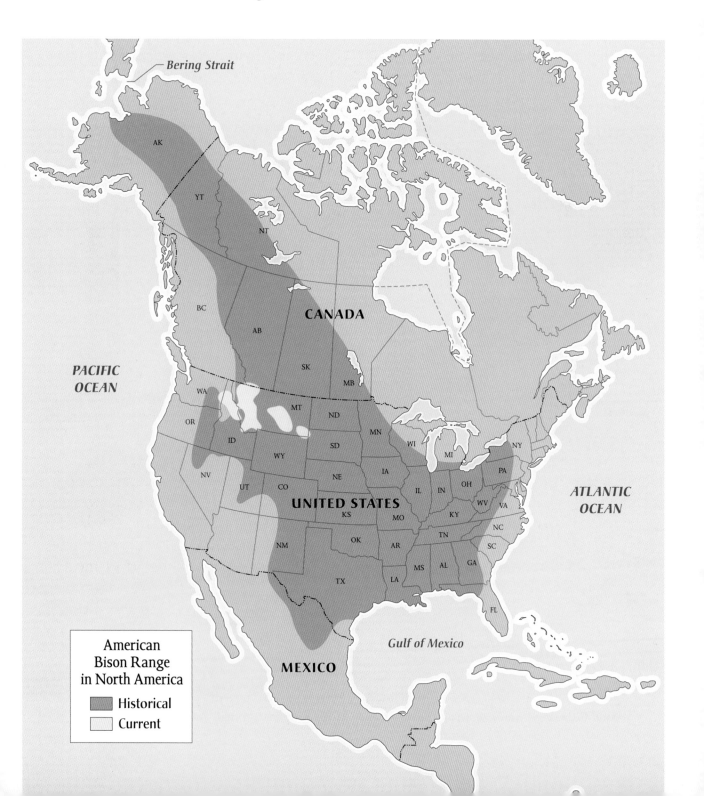

Bering Strait

PACIFIC OCEAN

ATLANTIC OCEAN

CANADA

UNITED STATES

MEXICO

Gulf of Mexico

AK

YT

NT

BC

AB

SK

MB

WA

OR

MT

ND

MN

WI

MI

NY

ID

SD

WY

IA

PA

NV

NE

IL

IN

OH

WV

VA

UT

CO

KS

MO

KY

NC

NM

OK

AR

TN

SC

TX

LA

MS

AL

GA

FL

American Bison Range in North America

■ Historical
□ Current

Bison are constantly on the move. They **migrate** in groups called herds. They usually travel about 2 miles (3 km) a day. Bison cover more land when searching for water or if they become frightened. A frightened herd will run in a wild, panicky, grunting rush. Many animals that migrate are guided by their need to find suitable places to give birth to their young in the summer. They also need winter resting areas. These migratory animals travel back and forth to the same areas season after season, year in and year out. But bison don't follow a migratory pattern. They just keep wandering. No one can predict where a herd will turn up next.

A small bison herd wanders across Hayden Valley in Yellowstone National Park.

When bison sense danger, they will face it. They may run toward the threat.

DEFENSE SYSTEMS

Bison have ways of protecting themselves. In the grasslands, there is nowhere to hide. A bison's best defense is to run. At full speed, a bison can run 35 miles per hour (56 km/h) for half an hour. That is faster than a horse and rider's top speed.

When bison feel threatened, they may suddenly turn around on their slender legs to face their enemies. Then bison resort to using their own heads as weapons. When faced with an enemy, human or otherwise, bison lower their heads and charge.

Bison can smell trouble from a long distance away. Their sense of smell is much stronger than their senses of sight and hearing.

A bison's head is well protected. A bison's forehead is made of a double layer of bone. The bone is covered by skin that is 2 inches (5 cm) thick and fur that is 4 to 5 inches (10–13 cm) deep.

This protection is very effective. When a gun is fired at a bison's forehead, the bullet may just bounce off. It stuns the animal for only a moment.

Bison horns make effective weapons too. Antlers are shed every year. But horns are lasting growth. They are hollow. And they grow to be 22 to 26 inches (55–65 cm) long. From tip to tip, a bison's horn can measure 2.5 feet (0.8 m) across. A bison can use its horns to pick up a wolf. The bison can toss the wolf so high in the air that the fall alone will kill it. Many hunters and their horses have been gouged by bison horns. Bison have even killed some of them. But it is rare for bison to kill one another.

Bison horns curl outward and upward from the head. The horns are bones covered in a material that is similar to human fingernails.

Above and opposite: Bison may be larger than cattle, but bison don't need any extra land to graze. Bison eat a wider variety of plants than cattle do.

SEASONAL
SURVIVAL TASKS

IT IS SUMMERTIME ON THE PRAIRIE. YELLOW CONEFLOWERS AND PURPLE prairie clover add sparks of color to the land. A light breeze sways the long prairie grasses. Here and there, bison are grazing. They don't have cutting teeth in their upper jaws to help them bite off grass. Instead, bison eat by wrapping their tongues around a tuft of grass. They pinch the grass off between their tongues and lower teeth. They swallow their food practically whole.

Bison are **ruminants**. Ruminants have stomachs that have four compartments. The different compartments help them digest their food. Most of the grass bison eat is originally stored in the **rumen**. The rumen is the first compartment of the stomach. But some of the food goes directly to the second compartment, the **reticulum**.

When bison graze, they first hold food in their rumens. Digestion begins in the reticulum.

Eventually, all the bison's food goes to the reticulum. There, stomach juices and bacteria begin to break the food down and form it into a **cud**. When bison are resting, muscles in the reticulum push the cud back up to the bison's mouth. The bison chews the food. It gets mixed with saliva. Then the bison swallows the food again. It is digested some more. It passes through the rumen, the reticulum, and into the third and fourth stomach compartments–the **omasum** and the **abomasum**.

WALLOWING

Grazing and resting bison may seem peaceful. But a closer look shows that they are constantly under attack by flying, biting insects. The insects are feasting on bison blood. This feasting can be very itchy, so bison **wallow**. They fall to their knees. Then they lower their bodies to the ground. They roll to one side and stretch their front legs forward. Next, they kick all four legs backward, throwing dust or mud over their entire bodies. After bison have wallowed on one side, they stand up and do the same thing on the other side. Bison can't roll completely over. Some people think that their humps get in the way.

A bull looks back at a swarm of insects attacking its hump.

Fine, loose dirt is ideal for wallowing. Bison may paw the ground with their hooves and poke it with their horns. This clears away grass and loosens hard-packed soil. Dirt mounds in prairie dog towns are favorite wallowing spots for bison. The dirt chokes the insect and shields bison from their bites for at least a little while.

Above: Wallowing looks like fun. Bison take dirt baths to make insects stop biting them.
Left: A bison rolls in the dust of a prairie dog town.

Sometimes bison use the same wallowing sites over and over again. Then the ground gets worn down. It looks like a giant bowl. That is the perfect shape for catching and holding rainwater. Native Americans, pioneers, and animals of the plains often satisfied their thirst at these wallowing sites.

Left: A bison's hump prevents it from rolling over on its back.
Below: When a lot of bison wallow in the same place, their rolling scoops away dirt to form bowls. These bowls will hold water when it is available.

Bison herds do many things together. *Above:* Bison rest and graze together under a bright blue sky. *Opposite:* A herd crosses a river as a group.

BISON HERDS

DURING THE SUMMER MONTHS, A BISON HERD IS MADE UP OF cows, bulls, and calves. But from September through June, the herd breaks into many smaller groups. One type of group is made up of cows and calves. Another type is made up of bulls. Members of bull groups normally spend no more than 9 days together. Then they wander off. That means several bulls are always grazing and chewing their cud alone.

Cow-calf groups and bull groups each have at least one leader. Leadership in any bison group changes all the time. A cow with a calf usually leads a cow-calf group. Cows rarely fight for top-ranking positions. Sometimes they lock horns and shove one another around. But usually the leader in a cow-calf group is the cow that the others follow while grazing. A top-ranking cow with a calf is also likely to become the leader when all the groups come together in June.

Bull groups change often. That means there is always some sort of rearranging for a top-ranking position. Mature bulls often challenge one another. But size, age, and personality keep many bulls from actually doing battle. Challenges begin when one bull stares directly at another. That may be followed by horn shaking, snorting, wallowing, and roaring. The other bulls in the herd may gather around the challengers. At any time, a challenging bull may back down. He gives up the top-ranking position in the herd to his challenger.

Competing bulls stare at each other and stomp on the ground.

Bison communicate with body language. A raised tail *(left)* signals anger. A lowered head indicates a bison is ready for a fight.

COMMUNICATING

Bison have developed special ways of communicating. That helps them live together in a herd. For instance, the way a bull stands and stares communicates rank. The position of a bison's tail is a sign of the animal's mood. Bison tails are almost always in motion. They are used as flyswatters. And they swing back and forth when bison are playing, nursing, or preparing for battle. A relaxed bison has a relaxed tail. It hangs downward and swings back and forth to control pests. An angry or frightened bison's tail is held straight up in the air.

Bison also communicate through sounds. When bison play, they make snorting, belching, and sneezing noises. Bison that are cornered or trapped squeak by grinding their teeth. Bulls roar like lions, especially during the mating season. And cows call for their calves with soft-sounding grunts. Their grunts are answered by their calves' high-pitched grunts.

Bulls fight during the mating season.

Bison make a variety of sounds.

MATING

Beginning in late June and continuing through September, bison herds come alive. This time of year is called the **rut**. During the rut, bulls roar at one another. They fight one another. They fight for the chance to mate with cows. Only the most **dominant**, the strongest and boldest, bulls in each herd are successful.

Most cows are ready to mate by the time they are 2 years old. Cows are pregnant for about 9 months. They usually have their first calves when they are 3. Bulls may be ready to mate by the time they are 2 years old. But they have to compete with stronger and older bulls for that right.

A top-ranking bull in search of a mate walks toward a group of cows. He tosses his head back and forth and snorts. All the other bulls move out of his way. When he gets to the cows, the bull sniffs each one. He is trying to find out which cow is ready to mate. After sniffing a cow, the bull stretches out his neck. He points his nose upward. The bull performs what is called the **lip curl**. The bull is using the **Jacobson's organ** in the roof of his mouth. It helps him sense smells.

Once a bull chooses a mate, a form of courtship begins. This is called the **tending bond**. The bull keeps the cow separated from other dominant bulls in the herd. Bull and cow stand and graze next to each other. They often face the same direction. Tending may last for as little as a few minutes. Or it may last for as long as a few days.

Left: A bull sniffs cows. He is looking for a cow that is ready to mate. *Below:* Before mating, a cow (*left*) and a bull (*right*) stand together in a tending bond.

A bull in a tending bond roars. It is his warning to other bulls to stay away.

At any time, the bull can be challenged by other bulls. Challenges lead to loud roars and dusty wallowing by all bulls involved. Bulls competing for the same cow usually know one another's rank. Low-ranking bulls tend to back off after exchanging a few wallows and roars. But sometimes the bulls follow up their displays of rank with head-pounding, horn-locking fights. But these fights are usually short.

The victorious bull lets the cow know when he is ready to mate. If she is not ready, the cow just moves away. If she is ready to mate, she stands still. She allows the bull to mount her from behind. Mating usually takes place at night. And it usually lasts for just a few seconds. A bull might continue to tend a cow for a few hours or a few days after they've mated. Then he goes off in search of another cow. Bulls mate with as many cows as possible. But cows mate with only one bull a year.

GETTING THROUGH THE WINTER

By the time the rutting season ends, summer is turning to fall. Colorful prairie flowers dry into seed heads. The land glows with shades of gold and copper. In the wide-open grasslands, a few trees or natural formations provide protection. Grassland animals suffer through scorching heat in the summer. In the winter, they endure biting wind, cold, and snow. Bison are grassland animals. As temperatures start to drop, the bison grow plump. Their coats become woollier. The bison are preparing for the cold weather. Bison are protected from the weather by a double coat of hair. It is made up of a short, dense undercoat and a longer, coarser overcoat.

A bison's overcoat is thick. Its body heat is slow to melt snow.

Soon snowflakes drift over the land. At times, snow buries the grasslands many feet deep. Ice forms on lakes and streams. But bison still need to eat and drink. They swing their heads from side to side. This clears away snow down to the grass. Then the bison can continue grazing. They can use their hooves and noses to break through ice to get water. But sometimes they just eat snow. Bison are hardy animals. They can endure temperatures down to –50°F (–45°C). Sometimes the weather is particularly severe. Then they huddle together for protection.

A bison uses its big head to dig through the deep snow. It will find plants to eat and water to drink under the snow.

In winter, ice can form on the bison too. Ice has formed around these bison's noses and mouths in the winter cold.

Spring Arrives

The snow finally melts. The grasslands are a gloomy, grayish brown. But soon, green shoots make their way through last year's matted grasses. Bison begin shedding their long, woolly coats. Bison groom the mats of winter hair off their bodies. One of the ways they do this is by wallowing. They also rub against anything and everything they can find. They rub against rocks and trees. But shedding is not the most important spring event.

Whoops!

One early settler wrote about a time when bison came to rub against his log cabin. They rubbed until the whole cabin fell down. The settler said he barely escaped with his life. These days, people report seeing bison stuck on top of roadside posts. This may look alarming, but the bison are merely enjoying a belly massage.

Left: Bison have rubbed bark off this tree trunk. Some wiry bison hair is stuck to it.
Below: A bison rubs against a tree to rid itself of some of its winter overcoat.

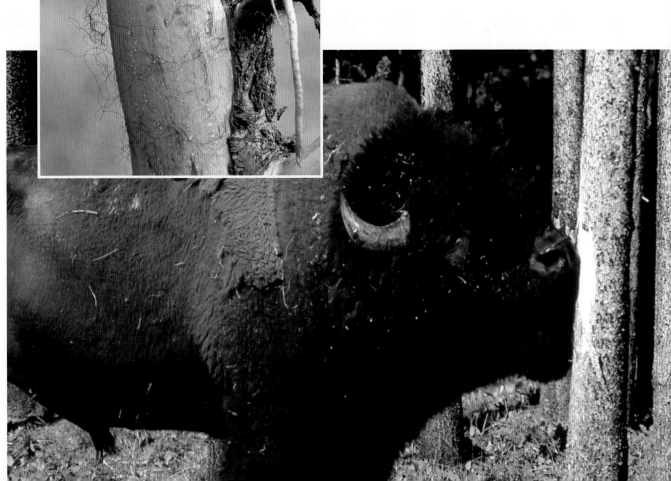

Above: These bison calves and their mothers live in Custer State Park in South Dakota.
Opposite: A bull sniffs a newborn calf. A newborn weighs 40 to 50 pounds (18 to 23 kg).

RAISING A FAMILY

SPRING IS THE TIME WHEN MOST COWS GIVE BIRTH TO THEIR calves. Cows can give birth to one calf a year. But they sometimes have only one calf every other year. Most calves are born between April and May. But some are born as late as October.

Giving birth to a calf is called **calving**. About 12 hours before calving, cows become nervous and restless. Sometimes they look for a quiet, safe, hidden place to calve. But other times, they just move to the outer edges of the herd.

It takes from 20 minutes to 2 hours to calve. Cows either lie on their sides or stand. When bison calves are born, their coats are a light brown color. The calves do not have humps or horns. They weigh about 40 to 50 pounds (18 to 23 kg). Just after birth, mothers lick their calves from head to hoof.

Within 10 minutes of being born, calves try to stand up for the first time. And within 30 minutes, most calves can stand. By the time calves are 3 hours old, they are running and romping around.

Often other herd members wander over to welcome new calves to the world. They lick and sniff the calves.

As soon as they are able to stand, calves try to **nurse**. Nursing is drinking the mother's milk from her **udder**. The calves' first attempts are not very successful. They often begin at the wrong end. They try to get a drink of milk from their mothers' necks. But soon, calves nose their way to their mother's udders. Then they greedily take their first drink.

Left: **A newborn calf works hard to get on its feet.**
Below: **Many calves first try to get milk from their mothers' necks.**

Above: A bison cow extends her tongue to her new calf. They are getting to know each other.
Inset: A calf nurses the correct way. Nearby, another adult in the herd watches out for the nursing pair.

Right after birth, calves and their mothers spend time getting to know one another. They use all their senses to do this. They memorize how the other smells, sounds, feels, and looks. This is called **imprinting**. It is a way for calves to develop close relationships with their mothers. It's the first step calves take toward learning how to live in a herd.

For the first 2 or 3 weeks of life, calves stay close to their mothers. By the third week, most calves roam as far as 50 yards (45 m) away. But if a cow becomes worried, she grunts for her calf. Then the calf quickly scurries back to safety and comfort. It begins to nurse. Cows with new calves are very careful. And this mood affects the whole herd. At any sign of danger, the cows may begin a stampede. The whole herd takes part in a stampede.

A growing calf trots after its mother.

Soon the number of calves grows. The calves' increasing independence becomes difficult for mother cows to handle. Sometimes the cows take turns watching a small group of calves. The other mothers can graze. Then the cows switch.

Calves begin nibbling on grass when they are 2 weeks old. Weeks and months go by. The calves eat more and more grass. If their mothers don't mate during the next rut, calves may continue nursing through their first year. But most calves are **weaned**, or no longer allowed to nurse, during their first winter.

As the year goes on, so does the growth of the calves. When calves are about 2 months old, their humps and horns begin to grow. Their voices deepen to a more adult tone. And their coats begin to darken. By the time the calves are 3 months old, they have the same chocolate brown coats that adults have. Calves spend more time with other calves. They chase one another, bucking and bounding and romping. Soon the rut begins again. Cows must turn their attention away from their calves and back to mating.

By the time calves are 1 year old, they weigh between 400 and 500 pounds (180–225 kg). Their horns have grown to a spiky 6 inches (15 cm). Soon the playing techniques of the **yearlings** will turn into skills for survival. They can do what is needed to keep themselves and the other herd members alive.

Calves, such as this one *(center)* begin to get humps and horns after they are 2 months old. At that time, their coats also begin to change from light brown to a darker adult brown color.

Above: A bison slows traffic in Wyoming.
Opposite: A bison appears to be headed to Yellowstone National Park.

BISON AND HUMANS

THE FIRST PEOPLE TO SHARE THE GRASSLANDS OF NORTH America with the bison were the Plains Indians. The Plains Indians of the 1700s and 1800s never settled into permanent homes. They were **nomadic**. They traveled from place to place. Bison were very important to the Plains Indians' way of life. Wherever the bison went, the Plains Indians followed.

The Plains Indians used almost every part of the bison's body. They ate the bison's flesh. They chewed the bison's nose cartilage for water. And they cooked pudding out of bison blood. They combed their hair with the rough side of the bison's tongue. They made clothes and shelter out of bison skins. And they even used the bison's organs as bags and containers. They carved tools out of bison bones. They burned bison droppings for fuel. They even played on sleds made from bison ribs.

The Plains Indians were successful hunters partly because they were bison experts. For instance, they knew that wolves would not hesitate to attack a single bison. But wolves would think twice before attacking an entire herd. As a result, healthy bison in a herd are not afraid of wolves. To hunt bison, the Plains Indians put on robes made of wolf skins. They crept up on a bison herd and killed the animals.

The Plains Indians also knew that bison would follow their leaders. Bison are driven to go with the herd. They don't always notice if there is trouble ahead. Hundreds of bison have often drowned because they followed their leaders onto thawing, ice-covered rivers. Native American hunters clothed in bison skins could lead an entire herd of bison right into a corral. Then they would kill the bison.

At one time, the Plains Indians did not have weapons that were strong enough to kill bison. The hunters would start a stampede, a sudden rush in one direction. They drove a whole herd over a cliff. Hundreds of bison were killed. But only some of the bison would be used by the Plains Indians. They had to do this to survive.

Left: **To sneak up to bison, some Native American hunters wore wolf skins. They moved on their hands and knees to get closer to the bison.** *Below:* **Sometimes the Plains Indians drove herds of bison over a cliff.**

Adult bison stand near a dead member of their herd.

SURVIVORS

When a bison is killed, some of the surviving herd members gather around the dead animal, nudging and sniffing it as though trying to bring it back to life. Sometimes the smell of blood stirs up a fight between bulls. These preoccupied survivors make easy targets for hunters, and in no time, they are killed as well.

AMERICAN SETTLERS AND AMERICAN BISON

Beginning in the late 1700s, the sight of countless numbers of stampeding bison also greeted the pioneers as they began to explore the land of a new nation called the United States of America. Wagon caravans carried settlers westward. They traveled through the Appalachian Mountains and across the Great Plains. That area was the home of the American bison.

Some people believe that the bison made it possible for pioneers to settle in the western wilderness. If not for the bison, many people might have starved or frozen to death. Bison were large, easy targets for the pioneers. The animals' bodies were used for food and clothing. In time, hunting bison became a favorite sport. As settlers spread across the United States, the bison population decreased. Before long, the bison were in danger of disappearing forever.

Europeans came to North America in the 1600s. They traveled across the continent in wagon trains to build settlements farther and farther west. Men shot bison for meat and fur clothing.

39

The newly arrived settlers used the same hunting methods as the Plains Indians. Both used herd behavior to drive bison into corrals or over cliffs. And both hunted with guns. The biggest difference was that the settlers hunted bison too much. In the mid-1800s, railroad tracks were laid across the plains.

The trains could carry settlers to their new homesteads. When engineers saw bison herds, they slowed their locomotives. They did this so travelers could stick their guns out the windows and shoot the bison. Rarely would engineers stop the train to pick up the bodies of the dead animals.

Hundreds of bison hides lie stacked. Early settlers killed a large number of bison.

Herds of bison sometimes stopped trains. A train's crew had to kill bison to clear the track. Other times, trains stopped to wait for bison to come close enough for passengers to shoot them just for fun.

The settlers had many reasons for hunting the bison to such an extreme. At first, the settlers' survival depended on the food and clothing that bison bodies provided. But soon, anything to do with the American bison became a symbol of danger and adventure. People began to kill bison for profit. Thousands of bison were killed for their tongues alone. (People considered bison tongues to be a fancy food in those days). The settlers also killed bison just because they caused trouble. Sometimes migrating herds crossed railroad tracks. The bison herds brought fast-moving trains to a complete stop. Or stampeding herds interrupted the progress of wagon caravans. And many settlers wanted bison off the rich prairie grasses so they could raise cattle and crops.

ALMOST EXTINCT

In less than 200 years, a land that once had 30 to 60 million bison was left with only about 500. These remaining bison were scattered in forested areas or kept on private ranches. By 1905, people feared that the American bison would become **extinct**, or die out completely. The American Bison Society was started. An effort was made to increase the bison population. The government set aside reserves where bison could be protected. They could live there without the threat of human hunters. Slowly, the bison population grew. By 1930, there were 4,000 bison. By the early 2000s, more than 250,000 roam U.S. and Canadian national parks and reserves and privately owned ranches.

A FEW TRIUMPHS

Bison continue to be part of Native American culture. On August 20, 1994, a snow white bison named Miracle *(below)* was born on the farm of Dave and Valerie Heider in Janesville, Wisconsin. The birth of a white bison is unusual, so the media covered the story. However, news of the birth spread especially fast among Native Americans. Miracle's birth fulfilled a 2,000-year-old prophecy of the Plains Indians.

The legend varies slightly from group to group, but the meaning is similar. According to Lakota legend, a young woman appeared in the shape of a white bison 2,000 years ago. She gave the Lakota ancestors a sacred pipe and sacred ceremonies. Before leaving, she told them that she would return to purify the world. She would bring spiritual balance and harmony. The birth of a white bison calf would be a sign that her return was at hand.

The odds of a white bison being born are estimated to be 1 in 10 million. The day after news

of Miracle's birth went out, Native Americans appeared at the Heider's farm. They asked for permission to see the calf, to pray to it, and to leave an offering. Soon the Heider's pasture and nearby trees were covered with offerings of feathers, necklaces, pieces of colorful cloth, and personal notes.

Since then, several other white bison calves have been born on various ranches. But they still remain something special.

Bison ranches are becoming quite popular. A growing demand for bison meat has made them a good investment economically. Many Americans have acquired a taste for bison meat.

Bison ranches also produce meat for sale throughout the world. If cooked properly, bison meat has a sweet taste and is quite tender. Nutritionally, it is lower in fat, cholesterol, and calories than beef or pork.

In modern times, the wild bison population is considered secure enough that hunting is again allowed if bison wander onto public lands. Still, the total number of American bison is only a fraction of one of the large herds that roamed the prairies in the 1800s. On the open plains, modern-day herds can number into the hundreds. But most herds have only about 30 members.

Right: **Packaged bison meat from a farm in Illinois**
Below: **Yellowstone National Park staff ride horseback to monitor a bison herd near Boiling River.**

GLOSSARY

abomasum: the fourth of a ruminant's four stomach compartments, where cud is combined with stomach juices before continuing on to the intestines

bull: an adult male bison

calving: giving birth to a calf

cow: an adult female bison

cud: partially digested food that is brought up from the bison's stomach to be chewed again

dominant: strongest and boldest

extinct: having no members of a species left alive

imprinting: a process that takes place soon after birth in which a calf uses its senses to recognize its mother and develop a close relationship with her

Jacobson's organ: an organ on the roof of a bison's mouth that combines the sense of taste and smell

lip curl: the curling of the upper lip that helps the tongue force scent to the Jacobson's organ

migrate: to move to a new living area for feeding or breeding

nomadic: traveling from place to place

nurse: to drink the mother's milk from her udder

omasum: the third of a ruminant's four stomach compartments, where chewed cud is further digested

reticulum: the second of a ruminant's four stomach compartments, where food is formed into a cud

rumen: the first of a ruminant's four stomach compartments, where most of the bison's food is stored after first being swallowed

ruminants: animals that have a three- or four-chambered stomach and regurgitate food as cud to chew again

rut: the bison's mating season, which usually lasts from June through September

subspecies: animals or plants of the same species with slight physical differences

tending bond: a temporary relationship between a cow and a bull that leads to mating

udder: organ containing a mother bison's milk

wallow: to roll around in dirt to relieve the itch of insect bites, to remove shedding fur, or as an expression of aggression

weaned: not allowed to nurse anymore

yearlings: 1-year-old bison

SELECTED BIBLIOGRAPHY

Danz, Harold P. *Of Bison and Man: From the Annals of a Bison Yesterday to a Refreshing Outcome from Human Involvement.* Niwot: University Press of Colorado, 1997.

Geist, Valerius. *Buffalo Nation: History and Legend of the North American Bison.* Stillwater, MN: Voyageur Press, 1996.

Haines, Francis. *The Buffalo: The Story of American Bison and Their Hunters from Prehistoric Times to the Present.* Norman: University of Oklahoma Press, 1995.

Hornaday, William Temple. *The Extermination of the American Bison.* Washington, DC: Smithsonian Institution Press, 2002.

Isenberg, Andrew C. *The Destruction of the Bison: An Environmental History, 1750–1920.* Cambridge: Cambridge University Press, 2000.

Lott, Dale F. *American Bison: A Natural History.* Berkeley: University of California Press, 2002.

Sample, Michael S. *Bison: Symbol of the American West.* Helena, MT: Falcon Press, 1987.

U.S. Fish and Wildlife Service. *American Buffalo: Bison Bison.* Washington, DC: U.S. Fish and Wildlife Service, 1995.

WEBSITES

American Bison (Buffalo)

http://www.amnh.org/nationalcenter/Endangered/

This website, maintained by the American Museum of Natural History in New York City, explains the endangered nature of the American bison—its status, habitat, and range—and what measures have been taken to protect it.

American Buffalo, Fresno Chaffee Zoo

http://www.fresnochaffeezoo.com/animals/bison.html

Maintained by the Fresno Chaffee Zoo, in Fresno, California, this site has information on the American bison, including a physical description, its scientific classification, behavior, adaptation, and more.

For Kids—National Bison Association

http://www.bisoncentral.com/index.php?c=14&d=109&a=1067&w=2&r=Y

This website, run by the National Bison Association, includes bison facts, coloring pages, and links to more resources.

Nature: American Buffalo

http://www.pbs.org/wnet/nature/buffalo/

This challenging website, created from the PBS show, *Nature,* has the history of the American bison, as well as links to puzzles, PBS videos, and more resources on American bison.

FURTHER READING

Marrin, Albert. *Saving the Buffalo.* New York: Scholastic Nonfiction, 2006.

Patent, Dorothy Hinshaw. *The Buffalo and the Indians: A Shared Destiny.* New York: Clarion Books, 2006.

Robbins, Ken. *Thunder on the Plains: The Story of the American Buffalo.* New York: Atheneum Books for Young Readers, 2001.

Swanson, Diane. *Buffalo Sunrise: The Story of a North American Giant.* 2nd ed. Toronto: Whitecap Books, 2007.

INDEX

ABOUT THE AUTHOR

While growing up in Minneapolis, Minnesota, **Ruth Berman** spent almost every Sunday at the University of Minnesota's agriculture campus playing with calves. She earned a B.A. in English and turned her love of animals into a career. She currently lives with her family in Riverside, California.

PHOTO ACKNOWLEDGEMENTS

The images in this book are used with the permission of: U.S. Fish and Wildlife Service, all page backgrounds, pp. 1, 5, 7, 15, 21, 27, 31, 37, 42, 44, 45, 46, 47, 48; © Jeff Foott/Discovery Channel Images/Getty Images, pp. 2-3; © SuperStock, Inc./SuperStock, p. 4; © Layne Kennedy/CORBIS, pp. 5, 17, 23, 25 (top), 32 (bottom), 33 (bottom); © Gustav W. Verderber/Visuals Unlimited, p. 6; © Karlene Schwartz, pp. 7, 16; © Laura Westlund/Independent Picture Service, pp. 8, 9; National Park Service Photo by Harlan Kredit, p. 10; © Prisma/SuperStock, p. 11; © PhotoDisc/Getty Images, pp. 12, 25 (bottom); National Park Service Photo by J. Schmidt, pp. 13, 19 (bottom); © age fotostock/SuperStock, p. 14; © Adam Jones/Visuals Unlimited, p. 15; National Park Service Photo by Jim Peaco, pp. 18 (top), 28 (top), 33 (top), 34, 37, 43 (bottom); © William Grenfall/Visuals Unlimited, p. 18 (bottom); National Park Service Photo by William S. Keller, p. 19 (top); © Steve Maslowski/Visuals Unlimited, p. 20; © John McDonald/Visuals Unlimited, p. 21; © Henry, P./Peter Arnold, Inc., p. 22; © Ingo Arndt/Minden Pictures/Getty Images, p. 24 (top right); © Gerald & Buff Corsi/Visuals Unlimited, p. 24 (bottom left); © Sarah Leen/National Geographic/Getty Images, p. 26; © William Albert Allard/National Geographic/Getty Images, p. 28 (bottom); National Park Service Photo by Jo Suderman, p. 29 (top); National Park Service Photo by Ed Austin/Herb Jones, p. 29 (bottom); © North Wind Picture Archives, pp. 30, 38 (both), 39 (bottom); © J. Mallwitz/Peter Arnold, Inc., p. 31; © Yann Arthus-Bertrand/CORBIS, p. 32 (top); © Panoramic Images/Getty Images, p. 35; © Daniel Lamoreaux/Visuals Unlimited, p. 36; © Woodfall Wild Images/Alamy, p. 39 (top); National Park Service Photo by J.R. Douglass, p. 40; Library of Congress, p. 41 (LC-USZ62-133890); AP Photo/Janesville Gazette, p. 42; AP Photo/James A. Finley, p. 43 (top).

Front Cover: © James Hager/Robert Harding World Imagery/Getty Images.
Back Cover: U.S. Fish and Wildlife Service.